Tragic Loves

30 real cases of crimes of passion

Phillips Tahuer

Ediciones Afrodita

Content:

1. The case of O.J. Simpson

In the heart of Los Angeles, a vibrant city full of movie stars lived three people whose lives were intertwined by destiny.

O.J. Simpson (1947-2024), known to many as "The Juice", was a man who had achieved glory both on the football field and on the big screen. His charisma, talent, and success had given him an almost mythical status in American society. However, behind his charming smile, there was a man whose personal relationships were full of conflict and darkness.

Nicole Brown Simpson (1985–1994), O.J.'s ex-wife, was a beautiful and vibrant woman, and mother of her two children, Sydney and Justin. Nicole had endured years of a tumultuous marriage, marked by episodes of domestic violence that ultimately led to her divorce in 1992. Despite her separation, the specter of O.J. continued to stalk his life.

Ron Goldman, a friendly young waiter, had become Nicole's friend. On June 12, 1994, he went to her house to return a pair of sunglasses she had left at the restaurant where she worked, an act of kindness that would seal her fate.

On that fateful summer night, Nicole and Ron were brutally murdered in the driveway of Nicole's Brentwood home. The bodies were discovered shortly after 10:30 p.m., presenting multiple stab wounds, in a scene that reflected a desperate struggle.

Police soon turned their attention to O.J. Simpson, Nicole's ex-husband, whose relationship with her had been stormy and violent. The evidence began to pile up: a bloody glove found on his property matched one left at the crime scene, and there were blood stains on her car and his house.

On June 17, 1994, the entire world witnessed one of the most iconic chases in history. O.J. Simpson, in a white Ford Bronco driven by his friend Al Cowlings, was chased by police as millions of people watched live on television. The chase ended in front of Simpson's home, where he eventually surrendered to police.

The trial of O.J. Simpson, which began on January 24, 1995, became an unprecedented media spectacle. Simpson's defense team, dubbed the "Dream Team," was composed of renowned attorneys such as Robert Shapiro, Johnnie Cochran, F. Lee Bailey, Alan Dershowitz, and Robert Kardashian.

The prosecution, led by Marcia Clark and Christopher Darden, presented compelling evidence: Simpson's DNA at the crime scene, the bloody glove, and shoe prints that matched those of O.J. However, the defense argued that the evidence had been manipulated and planted by police due to racial bias. One of the most dramatic moments of the trial was when O.J. tried to put on the bloody glove in court, and it didn't seem to fit, prompting Johnnie Cochran to proclaim: "If it doesn't fit, you must acquit."

On October 3, 1995, after 11 months of trial and only four hours of deliberation, the jury found O.J. Simpson not guilty of murder charges. The decision surprised many and divided public opinion, generating an intense debate about justice and racial problems in the United States.

Despite being acquitted in the criminal trial, Simpson faced a civil trial in 1997, where he was found responsible for the deaths of Nicole Brown Simpson and Ron Goldman. He was ordered to pay $33.5 million to the victims' families.

Simpson was never able to recapture his old life of fame and success. In 2007, he was arrested and convicted in an armed robbery and kidnapping case in Las Vegas, which resulted in a prison sentence. He was released in 2017. In April 2024 he died in Las Vegas due to the cancer he suffered from.

The case of O.J. Simpson remains one of the most famous and polarizing trials in American history. His outcome left deep scars on society, raising questions about the justice system, racism, and the power of the media. Through this tragic and complicated story, the figure of O.J. Simpson remains a symbol of the complexity and contradictions of human nature.

2. The case of Scott Peterson

In the quiet town of Modesto, California, she lived a young couple who seemed to have it all.

Scott Peterson (1972) was an attractive and charismatic man, who worked as a fertilizer salesman. Scott, with his impeccable appearance and social skills, had a life that many would envy. However, behind his facade, Scott led a double life that would soon fall apart.

Laci Peterson (1997-2002), a beautiful and vibrant woman, was pregnant with her first child. Laci was loved by all who knew her; Her infectious energy and her love for life illuminated the lives of those around her. She and Scott had married in 1997 and lived in a charming house in Modesto, where they eagerly awaited the arrival of their son, whom they had already named Conner.

On December 24, 2002, on Christmas Eve, Laci disappeared. Scott reported to police that he had last seen his wife that morning before going fishing at the Berkeley Marina. According to Scott, when she returned home, Laci was gone and he found her dog, McKenzie, wandering around alone with the leash still on.

News of Laci's disappearance spread quickly and the Modesto community mobilized to search for her. Extensive searches were conducted in nearby parks, neighborhoods, and rural areas. Images of Laci, with her radiant smile and her prominent pregnant belly, appeared in media outlets across the country.

As searches continued, police began to focus their attention on Scott. His demeanor seemed unusually calm for someone whose pregnant wife was missing. Additionally, disturbing details about his personal life began to emerge. Police discovered that Scott had been having an affair with a woman named Amber Frey, who was unaware of Scott's marital status, much less that his wife was pregnant.

Amber, upon learning of Laci's disappearance, contacted the police and became a key player in the investigation. She recorded her conversations with Scott, in which he continued to lie about her marital situation.

On April 14, 2003, nearly four months after Laci disappeared, two bodies were found in San Francisco Bay, near the spot where Scott had said she went fishing the day Laci disappeared. One of the bodies was a male fetus, almost fully developed, and the other was the severely decomposed body of a woman, later identified as Laci Peterson.

Scott Peterson was arrested on April 18, 2003, near a golf course in La Jolla, California. He was carrying $15,000 in cash, several identification cards, clothing, camping equipment, and dyed blonde hair, suggesting she may be planning to flec.

Scott Peterson's trial began in June 2004 and attracted enormous media attention. Prosecutors argued that Scott had murdered Laci and her unborn child, Conner, to free himself from his family responsibilities and continue his relationship with Amber Frey. They presented circumstantial evidence that included recordings of conversations between Scott and Amber, the trail of lies told by Scott, and his suspicious behavior following Laci's disappearance.

Scott's defense claimed there was no direct evidence linking him to the murders and suggested Laci may have been the victim of a kidnapping by strangers.

On November 12, 2004, after five months of trial and seven days of deliberations, the jury found Scott Peterson guilty of the first-degree murder of Laci and the second-degree murder of Conner. He was sentenced to death on March 13, 2005.

In 2020, the California Supreme Court overturned his death sentence due to errors in jury selection but upheld his conviction for murder. A new trial is pending to determine his sentence.

The tragic case of Scott and Laci Peterson is a grim reminder of how appearances can be deceiving and how violence can irrevocably destroy lives. Laci and her unborn son, Conner, are fondly remembered by family and friends, while Scott remains in prison, waiting for justice to take its course. The Petersons' story is a testament to the devastation that betrayal and violence can cause and continues to resonate in America's collective consciousness.

3. The case of Chris Watts

In the sleepy town of Frederick, Colorado, lived a family who, at first glance, seemed to be the epitome of domestic bliss.

Chris Watts (1985) was a hard-working man, with an apparently calm personality and dedicated to his family. He worked in the oil and gas industry and was known by his community as a devoted husband and father.

Shanann Rzucek (1984-2018) was a vibrant and dynamic woman, active on social media where she enthusiastically shared details about her family and professional life. She worked for a multi-level marketing company and was very loved by her friends and family. Shanann and Chris had two young daughters, Bella and Celeste, and were expecting their third child, whom they planned to name Niko.

On August 13, 2018, this seemingly happy family's life fell apart. Shanann, who had returned home from a work trip at 1:48 a.m., disappeared along with her two daughters. Chris, upon returning from work that same day, called the police after being unable to locate his wife and his daughters.

The community quickly rallied around the search for Shanann, Bella, and Celeste. Police began investigating, and Chris appeared in the media pleading for the safe return of his family. However, his behavior in front of the cameras and during interrogations raised suspicions.

Chris allowed investigators to search his home and, during this process, several inconsistencies in his story were found. Detectives noted that Chris did not display the expected emotions of a distraught husband and father.

On August 15, two days after the disappearance, Chris failed a polygraph test. Under pressure from interrogations, he confessed to having killed Shanann. However, he initially blamed her wife for murdering their daughters, claiming that he killed her in a fit of rage upon discovering what she had done.

Later, the most shocking truth came to light. Chris confessed to strangling Shanann at his house. Then, he loaded her body and her two daughters, still alive, into his truck and drove to a safe place for him. There, he murdered his daughters Bella and Celeste before disposing of their bodies in oil tanks and burying Shanann in a shallow grave.

During the investigation, it was discovered that Chris was having an affair with a co-worker, Nichol Kessinger. Apparently, the extramarital affair and his desire to start a new life without the responsibilities of a family were the reasons behind the horrible crimes.

On November 6, 2018, Chris Watts pleaded guilty to the murders of Shanann, Bella, Celeste, and Niko to avoid the death penalty. On November 19, he was sentenced to five consecutive life sentences without the possibility of parole, plus an additional 84 years for other crimes related to the murders.

The case of Chris Watts shocked the nation, generating a wave of sadness, outrage, and scrutiny over the appearance of normality for families. The tragedy of Shanann, Bella, Celeste, and Niko was a heartbreaking reminder of how betrayal and violence can hide behind a façade of happiness.

4. The case of Oscar Pistorius

In the bustling city of Pretoria, South Africa, lived a man who had achieved the status of a national hero.

Oscar Pistorius (1986), known as "Blade Runner" for the carbon-fiber prosthetics that he used to run, was a Paralympic and Olympic athlete who captured the hearts of millions with his impressive determination and sporting achievements. Pistorius, who had suffered the amputation of both legs since he was a baby, became a symbol of improvement and hope.

Reeva Steenkamp (1983-2013) was a promising model and lawyer. Known for her beauty and intelligence, Reeva had forged a successful career in the modeling world and had a strong presence in the South African media. She and Oscar began dating in 2012, forming a couple who often appeared in the pages of magazines and at social events.

On the night of February 13-14, 2013, in Oscar Pistorius' elegant home in a gated residential complex, a tragic event occurred that would change the lives of everyone involved. Pistorius had requested emergency services and then had spoken to a friend by telephone to inform him of the events. When police arrived, they found Reeva dead on the bathroom floor. Pistorius was arrested and charged with murder.

Oscar had fired four shots through the closed bathroom door, killing Reeva. According to Oscar, he thought an intruder had broken into his house and acted in self-defense. However, police and prosecutors painted a different picture, suggesting the shooting was the result of a heated argument between the couple.

The news of Oscar Pistorius' arrest shook South Africa and the entire world. Many refused to believe that the beloved athlete could be involved in such a tragedy.

The trial of Oscar Pistorius began on March 3, 2014, and became a media event followed by millions of people around the world. The prosecution, led by Gerrie Nel, argued that Pistorius had killed Reeva in a fit of rage after an argument. They presented evidence that included testimony from neighbors who heard screams before the shooting and text messages showing tensions in the couple's relationship.

Pistorius, for his part, maintained his version of events, stating that he had mistaken Reeva for an intruder. During the trial, he became emotional and cried on several occasions, describing how he was devastated by the loss of his loved one.

On September 12, 2014, Judge Thokozile Masipa found Pistorius not guilty of premeditated murder, but guilty of manslaughter (without intent to kill). On October 21, 2014, he was sentenced to five years in prison for Reeva's death and an additional three years, suspended, for reckless use of a firearm in another incident.

However, this was not the end of the case. The prosecution appealed the verdict, arguing that the sentence was too lenient and that Pistorius should have been convicted of murder. In December 2015, South Africa's Supreme Court of Appeal overturned the manslaughter conviction and found Pistorius guilty of murder, arguing that he should have known that gunshots through the bathroom door could kill someone.

On July 6, 2016, Pistorius was sentenced to six years in prison for murder. However, in November 2017, the sentence was increased to thirteen years and five months after another appeal by the prosecution.

The Oscar Pistorius case had a profound impact on South Africa and the entire world. The image of the disgraced hero resonated in the public consciousness, raising serious questions about domestic violence, gun control, and the justice system.

Reeva Steenkamp was remembered as a talented and brilliant woman whose life was tragically cut short. Her family has worked tirelessly to keep her memory alive and to advocate for victims of gender-based violence.

5. The case of Phil Hartman

In the world of entertainment, few names shined as brightly as Phil Hartman in the 1990s.

Phil Hartman (1948-1998) was a talented comedian, actor, and screenwriter, known for his versatility and charisma. Born in Brantford, Ontario, Canada, and raised in the United States, Hartman became a star thanks to his work on iconic television shows such as "Saturday Night Live" (SNL) and "NewsRadio." On SNL, he was famous for his impersonations of public figures such as Bill Clinton and his ability to take on a wide range of personas, earning him the nickname "The Glue" of the show.

Brynn Omdahl (1987-1998) born Vicki Jo Omdahl, was Phil's wife. Brynn was a former model and aspiring actress who had struggled to find her place in the entertainment industry. The two met in 1986 and married in 1987. The couple had two children, Sean and Birgen, and lived in a beautiful home in Encino, California. Despite the appearance of a perfect family life, Brynn struggled with personal problems, including addictions and jealousy of her husband's success.

On May 28, 1998, the quiet façade of the Hartman home was irrevocably shattered.

That night, Phil and Brynn attended a dinner with friends. After returning home, Phil went to sleep while Brynn went out again, apparently to continue drinking. She returned home late, intoxicated, and in an altered emotional state.

Around 2:00 a.m., Brynn, in a fit of rage and under the influence of alcohol and cocaine, entered the bedroom where Phil was sleeping and shot him three times, killing him instantly. Brynn then left the house and went to visit her friend Ron Douglas, to whom she confessed the crime. Initially, Ron didn't believe her, but when they returned to the house together, he found Phil's body and called the police.

When police arrived on the scene, Brynn barricaded herself in the bedroom with Phil's body. Moments later, she shot herself, ending her life and leaving her children without parents.

The news of Phil Hartman's death and the tragic circumstances surrounding it shook the entertainment industry and the public at large. Phil Hartman was a beloved figure, and his sudden and violent death left many in shock and sadness.

Phil and Brynn's children, Sean and Birgen, were placed under the guardianship of Brynn's sister, Katherine Kay Wright, and her husband Mike. The Hartmans' tragedy left a deep scar on all who knew and loved them.

Despite his tragic end, Phil Hartman's legacy lives on. His work on "Saturday Night Live" and "NewsRadio" continues to be celebrated, and he is remembered as one of the most talented comedians of his generation. His ability to transform into a variety of characters and his unmatched sense of humor left an indelible mark on comedy.

6. The case of Jodi Arias

In the quiet suburb of Mesa, Arizona, in 2008, a story of love and violence unfolded that captured the attention of the entire nation.

Jodi Arias (1980) was a young and attractive woman, born in Salinas, California. With a charismatic personality and a seemingly normal life, Jodi had artistic aspirations and worked as a photographer. However, behind her outward appearance, there was a woman with a history of turbulent relationships and a life marked by emotional conflict.

Travis Alexander (1977-2008) was a charismatic and successful man, known for his work as a motivational salesman and his active participation in the Church of Jesus Christ of Latter-day Saints (Mormon). Born in Riverside, California, Travis had overcome a difficult childhood and become an example of success and perseverance. Known for his friendly nature and ability to inspire others, Travis lived in Mesa, Arizona, and enjoyed an active social life.

Jodi and Travis met at a work conference in Las Vegas in September 2006. From that moment on, they began an intense romantic relationship, marked by emotional ups and downs and conflicts. Despite their differences, the relationship continued over the years, with passionate encounters and frequent breakups. Travis, deeply immersed in his Mormon faith, was often torn between his attraction to Jodi and her religious convictions.

On June 4, 2008, Jodi and Travis' relationship culminated in an unimaginable act of violence. Jodi traveled from California to Travis' home in Mesa. Although the exact details of what happened that night are up for debate, what is certain is that Travis was brutally murdered. His body was found days later by concerned friends, who found it in the shower of his house. He had been stabbed between 27 and 29 times, had his throat cut from ear to ear, and had been shot in the head.

The initial investigation quickly pointed to Jodi as a person of interest. Forensic evidence, including photos recovered from a digital camera showing images of Jodi and Travis together on the day of the murder, as well as photos of a bloodied Travis himself, incriminated Jodi. Additionally, Jodi's DNA was found at the crime scene.

Jodi was arrested on July 15, 2008, and during interrogations, she presented several versions of events. Initially, she denied being at Travis' house on the day of the murder. Later, she claimed that two intruders had broken into her home and killed Travis, but left her alive. Eventually, she admitted to killing Travis but claimed that she did it in self-defense.

The trial of Jodi Arias began in January 2013 and quickly became a media spectacle, followed closely by millions of people. The prosecution, led by Juan Martínez, argued that Jodi had planned the murder with premeditation, motivated by jealousy and rejection after discovering that Travis wanted to end the relationship and move on with her life.

The defense, on the other hand, portrayed Jodi as a victim of physical and emotional abuse at the hands of Travis, claiming that she had acted in self-defense during a violent attack. Jodi testified for 18 days, detailing her relationship with Travis and describing alleged episodes of abuse.

On May 8, 2013, the jury found Jodi Arias guilty of first-degree murder. The sentencing phase was complicated and extended over several months. The jury failed to reach a consensus on the death penalty, resulting in a mistrial at the sentencing phase.

In April 2015, Jodi Arias was sentenced to life in prison without the possibility of parole. The sentencing brought some closure for Travis' family and friends, but the impact of the case left a lasting mark on everyone involved.

7. The case of Clara Harris

In the town of Friendswood, Texas, a family seemed to have everything they needed to be happy.

Clara L. Suárez (1958), better known as Clara Harris, is a woman of Colombian origin who was married to 44-year-old David Lynn Harris. She was a successful dentist, known for her beauty and her ambition. Clara had worked hard to build a thriving career in the field of dentistry and owned several dental clinics. Her dedication and work ethic have made her a respected figure in her community.

David Harris (1958-2002) was also a successful dentist, working alongside his wife in his clinics. David and Clara married in 1992 and had two children. Apparently, they lived a comfortable and happy life in the suburbs of Houston. However, behind the façade of success and happiness, tension was developing that would culminate in tragedy.

In July 2002, Clara discovered that David was having an affair with a former beauty queen named Gail Bridges. The revelation was devastating for Clara, who had dedicated much of her life to building a family and business with David. Feeling that her world was falling apart, Clara hired a private detective to confirm her suspicions and obtain evidence of her husband's infidelity.

It didn't take long for the private detective to find the evidence. David and Gail were captured on video and photographs hugging and kissing at various locations, including the Nassau Bay Hilton hotel, where Clara and David had married ten years earlier.

On July 24, 2002, a heartbroken Clara decided to confront David and Gail at the Hilton hotel where they were staying. Clara brought with her her stepdaughter, Lindsey Harris, 16, David's daughter from her first marriage. Upon arriving at the hotel, Clara found David and Gail in the lobby, behaving affectionately. Clara's anger boiled over.

After a verbal and physical confrontation with Gail in the hotel lobby, Clara stormed out and headed to her car, a Mercedes-Benz S-Class. Lindsey watched in horror as the situation quickly deteriorated. In a fit of blind rage, Clara got into the car and ran over David in the hotel parking lot. Not satisfied with the initial impact, Clara turned around and walked over David's body two more times, making sure he was dead.

Clara was arrested at the scene and faced murder charges. The case attracted enormous media attention, in part due to the brutality of the act and the circumstances surrounding it. The prosecution argued that Clara had acted with premeditation and that her act of revenge had been deliberate and calculated.

The trial of Clara Harris began in January 2003. The defense portrayed Clara as a betrayed and emotionally devastated woman who had acted in a moment of temporary insanity. They argued that Clara had not planned to kill David, but that it had been an impulsive act brought on by rage and pain from her discovered infidelity.

The prosecution, on the other hand, used evidence from hotel surveillance video and the testimony of Lindsey, who had witnessed the crime from her car, to paint a picture of an act of cold-blooded murder.

On February 14, 2003, Clara Harris was found guilty of murder. She was sentenced to 20 years in prison and fined $10,000. The case became a reference point in the discussion about crimes of passion and their legal consequences.

During her time in prison, Clara kept a low profile and focused on her rehabilitation and her relationships with her children. In November 2017, after serving 15 years of her sentence, Clara was released on parole for good behavior.

8. The case of Betty Broderick

In the 1980s, in the sunny state of California, a story of love, betrayal, and revenge unfolded that captured the nation's attention.

Elizabeth Anne Bisceglia, known as Betty Broderick (1947), was an attractive and intelligent woman from New York. She grew up in an Italian-American Catholic family and was raised in an environment where marriage and family were central values. After meeting Dan Broderick at a party at the University of Notre Dame, they married in April 1969. Betty supported Dan while he attended medical school and then law school, working to support his family and raising their children.

Dan Broderick (1944-1989) was a charismatic and ambitious man who became a successful medical law attorney in San Diego, California. His professional success allowed the Broderick family to enjoy a wealthy lifestyle, with a beautiful home and all the amenities money could buy. However, behind the facade of success and happiness, the relationship between Betty and Dan is rife with tensions.

As Dan's career took off, the relationship between Betty and Dan began to fall apart. Dan began an affair with Linda Kolkena, his young paralegal. Betty, who had sacrificed her own career and youth for Dan's success, felt betrayed and furious upon discovering her husband's infidelity.

The divorce between Betty and Dan was long and bitter, marked by accusations, legal fights, and constant conflict. Betty accused Dan of manipulating the legal system in her favor, using her influence and knowledge to ensure that she received a minimum amount of money and restricted access to her children. The legal and emotional battle left Betty bitter and filled with anger.

On November 5, 1989, the situation came to a head. In an act of desperation and fury, Betty broke into Dan and Linda's house in the early hours of the morning. Armed with a gun, she entered the bedroom where Dan and Linda were sleeping and shot them both, killing them instantly. Betty then turned herself into the police, confessing to her crime.

Betty Broderick's trial began in October 1990 and became a media spectacle, attracting national attention. Betty's defense argued that she had been a loyal and self-sacrificing wife who was driven to the brink of desperation by Dan's emotional and legal abuse. They presented Betty as a woman who had been pushed to the edge by an unjust system and a traitorous husband.

The prosecution, on the other hand, argued that Betty had committed an act of premeditated murder, motivated by revenge and jealousy. They presented evidence that Betty had planned the murder, including the fact that she had taken the gun to Dan's house with the intention of killing him.

The first trial ended in a deadlocked jury, unable to reach a verdict. However, at the second trial in December 1991, Betty Broderick was found guilty of two counts of second-degree murder. She was sentenced to 32 years to life in prison with no chance of parole until 2010.

During her time in prison, Betty has maintained her version of events, stating that she was pushed to the edge by Dan's abusive behavior and the unfair justice system. Her children have had mixed feelings about her mother, with some supporting her and others condemning her actions.

In 2010 and again in 2017, she was denied parole. Her case continues to be a topic of public debate, with opinions divided over whether Betty is a victim of emotional and legal abuse or a ruthless killer who acted out of revenge.

9. The case of Stephanie Moseley

Stephanie Moseley (1984-2014) was a talented Canadian dancer and actress, born on February 14, 1984, in Vancouver. From a young age, Stephanie displayed exceptional talent for dancing and entertaining. She worked with numerous famous artists, including Britney Spears and Chris Brown, and landed a role in the television series "Hit the Floor."

Earl Hayes (1980-2014) was an American rapper and husband of Stephanie Moseley. Although he was not as well known as his wife, Hayes had worked in the music industry and had connections to several major hip-hop figures, including famous boxer Floyd Mayweather Jr., who was a close friend of his.

Stephanie Moseley and Earl Hayes married in 2008 and, at first, seemed to have a strong and loving relationship. However, over time, problems arose in their marriage. According to reports from friends and family, the couple had frequent arguments, many of which revolved around Hayes' jealousy and distrust of Moseley.

On December 8, 2014, the Los Angeles Police Department received calls reporting shots fired at the apartment complex where Stephanie and Earl lived. Upon arriving at the scene, they found Stephanie Moseley dead, with multiple gunshot wounds. Earl Hayes was also found dead, having shot himself in an apparent murder-suicide.

The tragedy unfolded amid reports that Hayes was deeply disturbed by suspicions that Stephanie had been unfaithful to him. On the night of the murder, Hayes had been speaking on the phone with his friend Floyd Mayweather Jr., who later reported that he attempted to dissuade Hayes from committing a violent act, but was unsuccessful.

Investigators concluded that Hayes had shot Moseley before committing suicide. The news shocked the entertainment community and the friends and followers of both, who could not understand how a relationship that seemed so promising ended in such a violent and tragic way.

In memory of Stephanie, many in the dance and entertainment industry have worked to raise awareness about domestic violence and the importance of seeking help before situations become tragic. Stephanie Moseley's story serves as a grim reminder of the dangers of abuse and despair when left untreated.

10. The case of Shayna Hubers

In the quiet suburb of Highland Heights, Kentucky, a story of love, obsession, and tragedy unfolded in the mid-2010s, capturing the attention of the media and the public.

Shayna Hubers was a 21-year-old young woman, intelligent and ambitious. She grew up in Lexington, Kentucky, and she excelled academically, earning a bachelor's degree in Psychology from the University there. After graduating, Shayna planned to continue her studies in graduate school, but her plans changed drastically when she met Ryan Poston.

Ryan Poston was a 29-year-old lawyer, known for his good looks and his professional success. He came from a wealthy family and worked at a law firm in Cincinnati, Ohio. Ryan had studied law at Indiana University and was known for his dedication and professionalism.

Shayna and Ryan met through mutual friends in 2011 and began dating shortly after. Although the relationship started strong, it soon became tumultuous. Ryan, described by his friends as a charming but reserved man, began to feel overwhelmed by his girlfriend's intensity. Shayna, for her part, became increasingly possessive and obsessed with Ryan, which caused constant conflict.

Ryan tried to end the relationship on several occasions, but Shayna always managed to convince him to continue. The relationship became a cycle of breakups and make-ups, with Shayna exhibiting increasingly erratic and controlling behavior.

On October 12, 2012, the situation came to a tragic end. That night, Ryan had a date with Audrey Bolte, a former Miss Ohio, which apparently angered Shayna. She went to Ryan's Highland Heights apartment, and after a heated argument, Shayna grabbed a gun and shot Ryan six times, killing him in her home.

After the shooting, Shayna called 911 and confessed to shooting Ryan, claiming she did it in self-defense. During the call, she displayed strange behavior, sometimes crying and other times speaking in a calm and emotionless manner.

Police arrested Shayna Hubers that same night. During interrogations, her fluctuating behavior raised suspicions. She claimed that Ryan had attacked her and that she shot him in self-defense. However, physical evidence and inconsistencies in her testimony suggested otherwise.

Shayna Hubers' trial began in April 2015. The prosecution argued that the murder was premeditated, motivated by Shayna's jealousy and obsession with Ryan. They featured text messages and emails in which Shayna showed her desperation to maintain the relationship. Additionally, the fact that Ryan had planned a date with another woman on the night of the crime was a key point in the prosecution's case.

Shayna's defense argued that she had acted in her own defense, claiming that Ryan was abusive and that Shayna feared for her life. However, forensic evidence, including the trajectory of the bullets and the positions of the wounds, did not support the defense theory.

In April 2015, Shayna Hubers was convicted of first-degree murder and sentenced to 40 years in prison. However, in August 2016, her conviction was overturned because one of the jurors had failed to disclose a previous criminal conviction.

In a second trial in August 2018, Shayna was again found guilty of first-degree murder and sentenced to life in prison with the possibility of parole after 20 years. During this trial, more details about Shayna's obsession and her manipulative behavior were revealed, reinforcing the conclusion that the murder was premeditated.

Following her conviction, Shayna Hubers has kept a low profile, serving her sentence in a Kentucky prison. She has continued to appeal her conviction, but so far, all of her attempts have been unsuccessful.

Ryan Poston's family has moved on, honoring Ryan's memory and advocating for justice for him. They have established scholarships in his name and have worked to raise awareness about relationship violence.

11. The case of Drew Peterson

In the suburb of Bolingbrook, Illinois, in the early 2000s, a story of mystery, manipulation, and tragedy unfolded that captured the attention of the entire nation.

Drew Peterson (1954) was a charismatic and seemingly respectable police sergeant for the Bolingbrook Police Department. Known for his charming personality and history on the force, Drew was also a man with a turbulent past in his personal relationships. He had been married four times, and his love life was marked by conflict and tragedy.

Stacy Ann Cales Peterson (1982-2004) was Drew's fourth wife. Much younger than him. Stacy married Drew when she was just 19 and he was 47. Despite the large age difference, the couple had two children together and seemed to have a normal family life. However, behind this facade, Stacy began to show signs of distress and fear.

Kathleen Savio, Drew's third wife, played a crucial role in this story. Before marrying Stacy, Drew had been married to Kathleen, and her marriage was also filled with problems. Kathleen and Drew had two children together, and their relationship ended in a bitter divorce filled with accusations of abuse and manipulation.

In 2004, Kathleen Savio was found dead in her bathtub, and her death was initially classified as an accident. The scene suggested she had slipped and hit her head, subsequently drowning in the bathtub.

However, Kathleen's family was always suspicious about the nature of her death, as she had repeatedly expressed her fear of Drew and had made clear in letters and conversations that she feared for her life.

Drew's life continued seemingly uneventfully until October 2007, when Stacy Peterson disappeared without a trace. Drew claimed that Stacy had abandoned the family, leaving him and his children. However, Stacy's friends and family did not believe this version. Before disappearing, Stacy had confided in her friends that she wanted to leave Drew and that she feared for his safety.

Stacy's disappearance led to a re-examination of the Kathleen Savio case. In 2007, her body was exhumed and a second autopsy was performed. This time, Kathleen's death was ruled a homicide, with evidence of a struggle and signs that she had been forced into the bathtub.

Stacy's disappearance and the new discovery of Kathleen's death put Drew Peterson at the center of an intense investigation. Drew maintained his innocence and denied any involvement in Kathleen's death or Stacy's disappearance.

In 2009, Drew was arrested and charged with the murder of Kathleen Savio. Drew Peterson's trial began in July 2012 and attracted considerable media attention. The prosecution presented a case based on circumstantial evidence, testimony from friends and family of Kathleen and Stacy, and Kathleen's prior statements about her fear of Drew.

A crucial piece of evidence was the testimony of a friend of Stacy's, who testified that she had told him that Drew had confessed to killing Kathleen and that she feared she would be his next victim.

In September 2012, Drew Peterson was convicted of the murder of Kathleen Savio and in February 2013 he was sentenced to 38 years in prison. During the trial, Drew showed little emotion and continued to proclaim his innocence.

Drew's conviction for Kathleen's murder brought no definitive answers about Stacy's disappearance. Although Drew has never been formally charged in Stacy's disappearance, many believe he was involved. Stacy's family has continued to seek justice and answers, keeping Stacy's memory and the hope of one day discovering the truth alive.

Regarding his life after the trial, Drew Peterson has continued to attract public attention even from prison. In 2015, he was accused of trying to hire a hitman to murder the prosecutor who had convicted him, adding more time to his sentence.

12. The case of Mark Hacking

In the summer of 2004, the city of Salt Lake City, Utah, was rocked by a story of love, deception, and tragedy that ended in a brutal murder.

Mark Hacking was a 28-year-old man, known for his charismatic personality and his ability to make friends easily. He grew up in a prominent family in Salt Lake City's Mormon community. Mark had presented a life of academic and professional success to his friends and family, although, in reality, he was hiding many lies.

Lori Kay Soares Hacking was a 27-year-old woman, loved by everyone for her kindness and generous nature. Lori worked as a manager at a Bed Bath & Beyond store and she was very excited about the future she was planning with Mark. They had been married since 1999, and Lori unconditionally supported her husband in her studies and professional plans. The couple seemed to have a happy and promising life.

On July 19, 2004, Mark called the police to report that Lori was missing. According to Mark, Lori had gone for a run in Salt Lake City Municipal Park and had not returned. This disappearance sparked a massive search involving the local community and the media.

As the investigation progressed, inconsistencies in Mark's story began to emerge. Friends and family revealed that Mark had lied about various aspects of his life. He had said that he had graduated from the University of Utah and that he had been accepted into the University of North Carolina School of Medicine, but investigations showed that he had never completed his bachelor's degree and had never been accepted into the university. School of Medicine.

The situation became even grimmer when it was discovered that Lori had learned about Mark's lies shortly before his disappearance. Lori had called the university and confirmed that Mark was not enrolled, which left her devastated.

On August 2, 2004, Mark Hacking was arrested after conclusive evidence was found of his involvement in Lori's disappearance. It was revealed that Mark had purchased a new mattress the same day he reported Lori missing and that he had disposed of the old one in a dumpster.

Under pressure, Mark confessed to his brother that he had killed Lori while she was sleeping, shooting her in the head with a rifle. He had then wrapped her body in garbage bags and taken it to the municipal landfill.

Mark's confession led to an intensive search of the landfill. On October 1, 2004, Lori's remains were found at the site, confirming the tragic truth. The autopsy confirmed that Lori had been murdered by a gunshot to the head.

Mark Hacking's case went to court, and in April 2005, he pleaded guilty to first-degree murder to avoid the death penalty. During the trial, more disturbing details were revealed about Mark's lies and the collapse of his fictional life.

The judge sentenced Mark to 6 years to life in prison. In Utah, this meant he would have to serve at least 30 years before being eligible for parole.

Following his conviction, Mark Hacking was transferred to Utah State Prison, where he continues to serve his sentence.

13. The case of Susan Wright

In the quiet suburb of Houston, Texas, in the early 2000s, a love story unfolded that transformed into a dark tale of violence and murder.

Susan Lucille Wright was a young mother of two children, known for her beauty and kindness. Born in 1976, Susan married Jeffrey Andrew Wright in 1998. The couple appeared to have a happy and stable life, with Susan playing the role of housewife and devoted mother, while Jeffrey worked as a carpet salesman to support the family.

Jeffrey, 34, was described by some as charming and gregarious, but he also had a dark side. He had problems with substance abuse and a volatile temper. According to later testimony, Jeffrey was often violent and abusive toward Susan, both physically and emotionally.

On January 13, 2003, Susan Wright reported to police that her husband was missing. She said Jeffrey had left the house and had not returned. However, just a week later, the truth began to emerge in shocking ways.

On January 18, 2003, police discovered Jeffrey Wright's body buried in the backyard of the Wright home. Jeffrey had been stabbed 193 times. Susan was arrested and charged with murder. During interrogations, Susan confessed to killing Jeffrey, but she claimed that she did it in self-defense, citing years of physical and emotional abuse.

Susan Wright's trial began in February 2004 and attracted considerable media attention due to the brutality of the crime and the nature of the abuse allegations. The prosecution argued that Susan had planned the murder of her husband with premeditation. According to them, Susan had tied Jeffrey to the bed under the pretext of sexual games and then stabbed him repeatedly before dragging his body to the backyard and burying him.

Susan's defense was based on allegations of domestic abuse. Susan claimed that she had endured years of physical and emotional abuse from Jeffrey and that on the night of her murder, she had acted in self-defense after he had attacked her. The defense presented testimony from family and friends that corroborated the abuse allegations.

One of the most shocking moments of the trial was when the prosecution recreated the crime scene in the courtroom. They used a bed and a mannequin to show how Susan had tied up Jeffrey and stabbed him, emphasizing the premeditated nature of the act.

In March 2004, Susan Wright was convicted of murder and sentenced to 25 years in prison. The jury partially accepted the prosecution's version of events, concluding that Susan had acted with premeditation and that the murder had not been an act of self-defense.

Susan's conviction was a devastating blow to her family, who firmly believed in her innocence and her account of years of abuse. In 2005, Susan appealed her conviction, and her sentence was reduced to 20 years.

During her time in prison, Susan Wright continued to maintain her innocence and fight for her freedom. In 2010, her case attracted renewed attention when the television show "Snapped" featured her story, generating renewed public interest and debate about her guilt and allegations of domestic abuse.

In 2014, after serving 11 years in prison, Susan Wright was released on parole. Since then, she has kept a low profile, focused on rebuilding her life and maintaining a relationship with her children.

14. The case of Michael Peterson

In the quiet town of Durham, North Carolina, in late 2001, a story of love, intrigue, and tragedy unfolded, capturing worldwide attention and becoming one of the most high-profile court cases of the time.

Michael Iver Peterson was a respected novelist and columnist, known for his political and social commentary. Born in 1943, Michael had served in the United States Navy during the Vietnam War and later devoted himself to writing. He was married to Kathleen Atwater Peterson, a successful Nortel Networks executive. The couple lived in a luxurious house in the Forest Hills neighborhood of Durham and seemed to have a perfect life, full of success and prosperity.

Kathleen, born in 1953, was an intelligent and hard-working woman, known for her kindness and dedication to her family. Michael and Kathleen had a blended family with five children from previous relationships, and together, they seemed to be the epitome of a happy, stable family.

The Petersons' seemingly idyllic life was shattered on December 9, 2001. That night, Michael called 911, reporting that he had found Kathleen unconscious and bleeding at the bottom of the stairs in his house. When paramedics arrived, Kathleen was already dead.

Michael claimed that Kathleen had accidentally fallen down the stairs after consuming alcohol and Valium. However, police and investigators found the scene suspicious due to the amount of blood and injuries on Kathleen's body, leading to further investigation.

Kathleen's autopsy revealed multiple injuries to her head, which medical examiners concluded could not have been caused by a simple fall. These injuries, along with the amount of blood found at the scene, led prosecutors to believe that Kathleen had been murdered.

In 2003, Michael Peterson was arrested and charged with the murder of his wife. The trial began in July 2003 and became a media circus, with the eyes of the public and the media focused on every detail of the case.

The prosecution presented a case based on circumstantial and forensic evidence. They argued that Michael had beaten Kathleen to death, using a blunt object. They also presented evidence about Michael's bisexuality, suggesting that Kathleen had discovered her sexual encounters with men and that this had led to a violent confrontation.

Michael's defense argued that Kathleen had died accidentally after falling down the stairs. They hired experts who testified that Kathleen's injuries could have been caused by a fall. They also presented evidence that Michael and Kathleen's relationship was loving and stable.

One of the most powerful moments of the trial was the testimony of Patricia, a close friend of Michael, and his first wife, Elizabeth Ratliff. Elizabeth had died in Germany in 1985 under similar circumstances, having been found dead at the foot of a staircase. This case was reopened and it was determined that Elizabeth had also been murdered, although Michael was never charged in connection with her death.

On October 10, 2003, Michael Peterson was convicted of first-degree murder and sentenced to life in prison without the possibility of parole. The conviction divided public opinion, with some believing in Michael's innocence and others convinced of his guilt.

Michael Peterson's story did not end with his conviction. In 2011, Michael's defense presented new evidence, arguing that the testimony of Duane Deaver, a key prosecution blood analyst, was unreliable. Deaver had been fired from the North Carolina State Crime Laboratory for misconduct, leading to a new trial.

In 2017, after spending more than eight years in prison, Michael Peterson accepted a plea deal, allowing him to plead guilty to involuntary manslaughter while maintaining his innocence. He was sentenced to time served and released.

After his release, Michael Peterson has kept a low profile, although his case remains the subject of debate and speculation. His story was documented in the Netflix series "The Staircase," which garnered worldwide attention and sparked new theories about Kathleen's death.

Kathleen's family continues to deal with the loss and controversies surrounding the case. Some members of Michael and Kathleen's family have supported Michael, while others are convinced of his guilt.

15. The case of Nancy Seaman

In the quiet community of Farmington Hills, Michigan, a story of love and horror unfolded in 2004, involving a couple who seemed to have it all, but whose marriage was filled with dark secrets and abuse.

Nancy Seaman was a 52-year-old elementary school teacher, described by her colleagues and friends as a kind woman, dedicated to her work and her family. Nancy had two adult children and had been married to Bob Seaman for over 30 years. The couple lived in a comfortable house in the suburbs, and from the outside, their life seemed idyllic.

Bob Seaman, 57, was a businessman who worked in the automotive industry. Although he was respected in his field, at home, Bob was known for having a volatile temper and for being controlling and abusive towards Nancy. Over the years, Nancy endured numerous incidents of physical and emotional abuse, eventually reaching a breaking point.

On May 10, 2004, Nancy Seaman attacked her husband Bob in the kitchen of her home, using an ax and a knife. Nancy hit Bob repeatedly with the ax and then stabbed him with the knife, causing fatal injuries. After the attack, Nancy attempted to clean up the crime scene and hide Bob's body in the garage, covering it with blankets and cardboard.

That same morning, Nancy went to the school where she worked and taught her classes as if nothing had happened. However, her behavior was unusually nervous and distracted, which caught the attention of her colleagues.

Later, Nancy went to a home improvement store, where she purchased cleaning products and other supplies to try to better conceal the crime. The store's security cameras captured Nancy purchasing these items, which became crucial evidence in the investigation.

Police were alerted after one of the Seamans' children failed to contact her parents and found the crime scene. When officers arrived at the house, they discovered Bob's body in the garage and arrested Nancy.

During interrogations, Nancy confessed to killing Bob, but she claimed that she did it in self-defense after he attacked her. Nancy described a pattern of abuse she had endured for years and said she feared for her life.

Nancy Seaman's trial began in October 2004. The prosecution argued that she had planned Bob's murder with premeditation and presented evidence of her purchase of the supplies as proof of her intention to conceal the crime. The defense, on the other hand, focused on Bob's history of abuse toward Nancy and argued that she had acted in self-defense of her.

One of the most shocking moments of the trial was when the defense presented witnesses and documents supporting allegations of abuse against Nancy. Friends and family testified about Bob's violent behavior and how she had endured years of abuse in silence.

In November 2004, Nancy Seaman was convicted of first-degree murder and sentenced to life in prison without the possibility of parole. The jury partly accepted the prosecution's version that the murder had been premeditated, rejecting her self-defense as sufficient justification for the crime.

Nancy's conviction was a devastating blow to her children and to those who believed her story of abuse. Many felt that the justice system had not adequately taken into account the history of domestic violence and the despair Nancy must have felt.

Nancy Seaman was sent to prison, where she continues to serve her sentence. Over the years, her case has attracted the attention of women's rights advocates and anti-domestic violence organizations, who argue that her conviction was unfair and should be reviewed in the context of the abuse she suffered. she suffered.

In 2009, Nancy Seaman's case was featured on the television show "Snapped," sparking renewed interest and debate about her situation. In 2010, a federal judge overturned Nancy's conviction, ordering a new trial on the grounds that her attorney had failed to provide an adequate defense by not presenting sufficient evidence of the abuse she had suffered. However, this decision was later reversed, and Nancy remains imprisoned.

16. The case of Barbara Sheehan

In the bustling borough of Queens, New York, in the spring of 2008, a love story that turned bitter and violent culminated in a trial that attracted national attention.

Barbara Sheehan was a mother of two children and a dedicated worker in the New York school system. Born in 1961, Barbara was known for her kindness and devotion to her family. For many years, she endured a difficult and abusive marriage to Raymond Sheehan, a retired NYPD sergeant.

Raymond Sheehan, also known as Ray, was a 49-year-old man who, despite his dedication to the police force, was known in the private sphere for his controlling and violent behavior. According to Barbara and her children, Ray had physically and emotionally abused Barbara for nearly two decades, creating an environment of constant fear in the home.

On February 18, 2008, Barbara's life took a drastic turn. That day, Barbara shot and killed Ray in his Queens home. She used two firearms, one of them belonging to Ray, and fired eleven shots at him while he was in the bathroom.

Barbara called her daughter immediately after the incident, who then alerted authorities. When the police arrived, they found Ray's body and arrested Barbara. During interrogations, Barbara admitted to shooting her husband, but she claimed she did it in self-defense after years of abuse and an immediate threat to her life.

Barbara Sheehan's trial began in September 2011. The prosecution argued that Ray's murder was premeditated and presented evidence suggesting that Barbara had planned the attack. They argued that Barbara had other options to escape the abuse, but she chose violence.

Barbara's defense focused on her history of domestic abuse. They presented testimony from friends, family, and experts that confirmed allegations of physical and emotional abuse by Ray. Barbara testified about the details of her abuse, describing numerous incidents in which Ray had beaten her, threatened her with weapons, and controlled her daily life.

One of the most shocking moments of the trial was the testimony of Barbara and Ray's children, who corroborated her mother's story and described the environment of terror in which they had lived. They claimed that her father had been extremely violent and that they feared for her mother's life.

In October 2011, the jury found Barbara Sheehan not guilty of second-degree murder, accepting her defense that she had acted in self-defense. However, she was found guilty of illegal weapons possession, as she had used Ray's weapons without having a license.

Barbara was sentenced to five years in prison on the charge of illegal weapons possession. This sentence was received with a mixture of relief and sadness by her family and advocates, who firmly believed in her innocence and her right to defend herself against herself after years of abuse.

Barbara Sheehan served her sentence in a New York prison and was released in 2017. During her time in prison, she continued to maintain her innocence and defend her right to have acted in self-defense.

Her case attracted the attention of women's rights advocates and anti-domestic violence organizations, who saw in Barbara an example of how the justice system often fails to protect victims of domestic abuse. Her story was featured on several television shows and documentaries, sparking debate about self-defense laws and domestic violence.

17. The case of Fadi Nasri

In the vibrant city of London, a tragic story of love and betrayal unfolded in 2006. The case of Fadi Nasri and his wife Nisha Patel-Nasri captured the attention of the British press, revealing a dark plot that ended in murder.

Fadi Nasri was a 33-year-old businessman and owner of a limousine rental company. Of Lebanese descent, Fadi was known for his lavish lifestyle and outgoing nature. He seemed like a loving and devoted husband.

Nisha Patel-Nasri, 29, was a volunteer police officer and owner of a successful beauty salon. Nisha was known for her dedication to the community and her passion for helping others. She was a vibrant and hard-working woman, much loved by her family and friends.

On May 11, 2006, Nisha was brutally stabbed outside her home in Wembley, north-west London. The police found Nisha seriously injured; she had been stabbed with her own kitchen knife. She was taken to the hospital, where she succumbed to her injuries shortly after.

The initial investigation suggested that she may have been the victim of a burglary gone wrong, as some belongings were missing from the home and the door had been forced open. However, as authorities delved deeper into the case, suspicions began to arise about her husband, Fadi Nasri.

Police soon discovered that Fadi Nasri was deeply in debt and that his limousine business was in financial difficulty. Additionally, it was revealed that Fadi was having an affair with another woman, a waitress named Ludmila Zikova. These revelations changed the direction of the investigation.

Detectives discovered that Fadi had hired a hitman to kill his wife in the hope of collecting a £350,000 life insurance to relieve his debts and continue his life with Ludmila. Police tracked down Fadi's accomplices, leading to the arrest of Roger Leslie, a known criminal who acted as an intermediary, and Jason Jones, the man who carried out the murder.

Fadi Nasri's trial began in January 2008. The prosecution presented a strong case against him, arguing that Fadi had premeditatedly and coldly planned the murder of his wife. They presented evidence of phone calls between Fadi and the co-conspirators, as well as financial details showing the motive behind the crime.

Ludmila Zikova testified at trial, revealing details about her relationship with Fadi and confirming that he had talked about getting rid of his wife so they could be together and resolve her financial problems. This testimony was devastating for the defense.

Fadi Nasri maintained his innocence, claiming that he had never wanted his wife dead and that conversations with Leslie and Jones had been misinterpreted. However, the evidence against him was overwhelming.

On May 28, 2008, Fadi Nasri was found guilty of murder and conspiracy to commit murder. He was sentenced to life in prison, with a minimum of 20 years before being eligible for parole. Roger Leslie and Jason Jones were also sentenced to long prison terms for their roles in the murder.

Fadi Nasri's conviction brought a sense of justice to Nisha's family and friends, although he could never repair the damage caused by her tragic loss. The community in Wembley was shocked by the brutality of the crime and the betrayal of someone so close to the victim.

Ludmila Zikova, Fadi's lover, distanced herself from the public eye after the trial. The lives of everyone involved changed dramatically, and Nisha's memory was honored through several vigils and tributes from the community she had served so much.

18. The case of Jason Young

In the quiet town of Raleigh, North Carolina, a seemingly perfect family was shaken by a brutal murder in November 2006. This case, known as the Michelle Young murder, involved family man Jason Young and became one of the most intriguing trials of the decade.

Jason Young was a 32-year-old businessman who worked in sales. He was known for his charisma and for being a seemingly dedicated husband and father. However, his frequent work trips and a troubled marriage were beginning to darken this image.

Michelle Young, 29, was a loving, hard-working mother who was pregnant with her second child. She was known for her kindness and dedication to her two-year-old daughter, Cassidy. Michelle had shared with friends and family that her marriage to Jason was not perfect and that there were tensions in her relationship.

On November 3, 2006, Michelle Young's body was found in her home by her sister, Meredith Fisher. Michelle lay in a pool of blood, brutally beaten to death. The scene was frightful; It seemed like Michelle had fought fiercely for her life. Her young daughter, Cassidy, was found unharmed but covered in her mother's blood, wandering around the house.

Jason Young, Michelle's husband, alleged that he was out of town for work at the time of the murder. He said he had spent the night at a hotel in Virginia. However, evidence soon began to point towards him.

The investigation revealed several incriminating details against Jason Young. Hotel security footage showed Jason had left the hotel around 1 a.m. and he had returned several hours later. Additionally, phone records indicated that his cell phone was turned off during the critical time of the murder, which seemed suspicious.

Jason's vehicle also came under scrutiny. Police found traces of mud on his tires that matched the type of dirt near the Youngs' home, suggesting that Jason had been in the area the night of the murder.

Jason's behavior also raised suspicions. Despite the brutal death of his wife, Jason seemed indifferent and remorseless. During interrogations and interviews with police, his cold and distant attitude fueled suspicions against him.

In 2009, almost three years after the murder, Jason Young was arrested and charged with the murder of his wife Michelle. The first trial in 2011 ended in a hung jury, unable to reach a unanimous verdict. However, the prosecution did not give up and a second trial was scheduled.

Jason Young's second trial began in February 2012. The prosecution presented circumstantial but compelling evidence, including hotel video recordings, phone records, and analysis of mud on his vehicle. He also presented testimony from Meredith Fisher, Michelle's sister, who described the crime scene and Jason's unusually cold demeanor after the murder.

Jason's defense argued that there was no direct evidence linking him to the murder and suggested that an unknown intruder could have committed the crime. However, the circumstantial evidence and lack of a solid alibi proved overwhelming.

On March 5, 2012, Jason Young was found guilty of the first-degree murder of Michelle Young. He was sentenced to life in prison without the possibility of parole. Michelle's family, especially her mother Linda Fisher, expressed relief and satisfaction at the verdict, although Michelle's loss left a permanent wound.

After his conviction, Jason Young continued to maintain his innocence and his lawyers appealed the verdict on several occasions, but all appeals were denied. The story of Michelle Young and her tragic murder has been the subject of several television programs and documentaries, exploring the details of the case and the complexities of the justice system.

Cassidy Young, Michelle and Jason's daughter was raised by Michelle's family, who made sure she grew up in a loving and safe environment. The tragedy of her mother's death and her father's conviction remains a shadow over her life, but Michelle's family has worked hard to provide her with as normal a life as possible.

19. The case of Robert Blake

On the Hollywood scene, few stories have been as dramatic and tragic as that of Robert Blake and his wife, Bonny Lee Bakley. This case became a media spectacle due to the fame of Blake, known for his career as an actor in series such as "Baretta."

Robert Blake was born Michael James Gubitosi in 1933 and had a long and successful career in Hollywood. He started out as a child actor in the short film series "Our Gang" and later became famous for his starring role in the television series "Baretta." Over the years, Blake cultivated a public image as a tough but likable guy.

Bonny Lee Bakley was a 44-year-old woman with a troubled past. Born in 1956, Bakley had had a complicated life, marked by multiple marriages and a history of celebrity scams. Bonny was known for her obsession with celebrities and her ability to manipulate situations to her advantage.

On May 4, 2001, Bonny Lee Bakley was found dead in Robert Blake's car, parked near Vitello's Italian restaurant in Studio City, Los Angeles. She had been shot in the head while she was waiting for Blake, who he claimed had returned to the restaurant to pick up a gun she had accidentally left there.

The relationship between Blake and Bakley had been tumultuous from the beginning. They met in 1999, and soon after, Bakley became pregnant. Initially, she claimed that the baby's father could be Christian Brando, son of famous actor Marlon Brando, but DNA testing confirmed that Blake was the father. They married in November 2000, but their marriage was turbulent and marked by mistrust and conflict.

Los Angeles police quickly zeroed in on Blake as the prime suspect. The circumstances of the crime, along with the history of conflict between Blake and Bakley, made police suspicious of Blake's version of events. Additionally, two of Blake's former stunt doubles, Ronald "Duffy" Hambleton and Gary McLarty, testified that Blake had offered them money to kill Bakley, although both refused.

During the investigation, more details emerged about the couple's complicated relationship. Bakley had kept his life full of deception even after marrying Blake, which increased tensions. Detectives also found that Blake possessed several weapons, although the gun used in the murder was not recovered.

Robert Blake's trial began in December 2004. The prosecution painted a picture of Blake as a man desperate to free himself from a wife who he felt had manipulated him into marrying him and who posed a constant threat. They used the testimonies of Hambleton and McLarty to argue that Blake had premeditated Bakley's murder.

Blake's defense, led by attorney M. Gerald Schwartzbach, argued that Blake did not have sufficient motive to murder his wife and that the accusations were unfounded. They also raised questions about the credibility of Hambleton and McLarty's testimonies, suggesting that both were seeking personal attention and benefits.

On March 16, 2005, after months of testimony and deliberations, the jury found Robert Blake not guilty of murder and one count of conspiracy to commit murder. However, the trial was not the end of Blake's legal problems.

In November 2005, Bonny Lee Bakley's children filed a civil lawsuit against Robert Blake for the death of their mother. In November 2006, a civil jury found Blake liable for Bakley's death and ordered him to pay $30 million to Bakley's children. This sentence was devastating for Blake, who had already spent a large portion of his fortune on his criminal defense.

Blake filed for bankruptcy in February 2006, claiming that he could not pay the amount ordered by the civil court. His career, which had once been a Hollywood success story, was completely destroyed. Blake withdrew from public life, and his reputation was irreparably damaged.

Robert Blake has maintained a relatively quiet life since the trial, largely avoiding media attention. Although he maintained his innocence, the civil trial verdict and public opinion tarnished his legacy. Blake passed away in 2023.

20. The case of Dan Markel

The murder of Dan Markel, a renowned law professor at Florida State University (FSU), shook the academic and legal community in the United States. The case was further complicated by revelations of family conflicts and conspiracies.

Dan Markel was born in Toronto, Canada, on October 9, 1972. After studying at Harvard and the University of Cambridge, he became a respected academic in the field of criminal law. Markel was known for his academic publications and his blog on criminal law. He was divorced from Wendi Adelson, with whom he had two young children.

Wendi Adelson, also a law professor at FSU, came from a wealthy and prominent Miami family. After a tumultuous marriage to Dan, they divorced in 2013, a year before the murder. The post-divorce relationship was conflictive, particularly regarding the custody of their children.

On July 18, 2014, Dan Markel was found in his car in the garage of his home in Tallahassee, Florida, shot in the head. He was rushed to hospital but died the next day due to serious injuries. The murder shocked the local community and the academy, generating an intense police investigation.

The initial investigation focused on Markel's professional and personal environment, as there were no signs of robbery or forced entry. The tips led police to take a closer look at his personal life, especially his tumultuous relationship with his ex-wife and his family.

The tensions between Markel and the Adelson family were well known. Wendi and her family, especially her brother Charlie Adelson and her mother Donna Adelson, had repeatedly expressed their desire for Wendi to move with the children to Miami, something which Markel had legally blocked.

The investigation took a significant turn when police discovered that two men, Sigfredo García and Luis Rivera, had traveled from Miami to Tallahassee in the days before Markel's murder. Security cameras and phone records linked these men to the crime scene.

Sigfredo García was discovered to be in a relationship with Katherine Magbanua, who in turn had ties to the Adelson family. Katherine was the mother of Siegfried's children and had been romantically involved with Charlie Adelson.

Luis Rivera, a member of the Latin Kings gang, accepted a plea deal in exchange for his testimony against Sigfredo García and Katherine Magbanua. Rivera confessed that he and Garcia had been hired to kill Markel and that the murder was planned by Katherine Magbanua and Charlie Adelson.

In October 2019, Sigfredo García was found guilty of first-degree murder and sentenced to life in prison. Katherine Magbanua was tried in 2019, but the trial ended in a deadlocked jury. In a second trial in May 2022, she was convicted of first-degree murder and sentenced to life in prison without the possibility of parole.

In April 2022, Charlie Adelson was arrested and charged with first-degree murder, conspiracy to commit murder, and solicitation of murder. His trial is pending.

21. The case of Karla Homolka and Paul Bernardo

Karla Homolka, a 17-year-old girl from a loving family, lived in Toronto, Canada, and one day she fell madly in love with a man who would drag her into a dark world of violence and perversion. It would turn out to be Paul Bernardo, 23 years old, charismatic and manipulative, who hid a sadistic obsession with control and sexual violence.

Their romance began in 1987 and soon the attraction turned into a dark complicity. Bernardo, consumed by his twisted desires, found in Karla an accomplice willing to please him. Together, they started a crime spree that would shock Canada.

Like every couple, at first, they lived it as a honeymoon, but as the months went by, Paul began to reproach her young girlfriend for telling her that when he met her she was no longer a virgin.

The fact that he was not her first man bothered Paul, who began channeling his sexual thoughts toward Karla's sister, Tammy, who was only 15 years old. For her part, Karla Homolka, willing to satisfy all the desires of her partner, orchestrated a plan for her future husband to satisfy her sexual desires.

Tammy Homolka, Karla's younger sister, was the first victim. Drugged and manipulated by her own sister, she was raped and then murdered by Bernardo. A macabre "birthday" gift for the monster who had turned her into his puppet.

Leslie Mahaffy and Kristen French, two young students, full of dreams and promises, were intercepted by the diabolical couple. Kidnapped, tortured, raped, and finally murdered, their bodies were discarded as if they were simple objects.

Bernardo's bloodlust knew no limits and his crimes intensified. However, the couple's façade was beginning to crack. Suspicions grew and Karla, fearing for her own life, decided to betray him.

In 1993, Homolka confessed to her involvement in the crimes in exchange for immunity from prosecution. She suffered from hybristophilia, a tendency to be attracted to people who have committed a crime, a crime, or have a propensity to commit it. Chilling recordings and home videos of her revealed the unimaginable cruelty of the acts committed by the couple. Bernardo, cornered by the evidence, was sentenced to life in prison without the possibility of parole.

Paul Bernardo and Karla Homolka were raped and murdered for two years, to which must be added the previous years in which he acted alone. A total of forty crimes are attributed to him, including rapes and murders.

The case of Karla Homolka and Paul Bernardo shocked the world. Karla's angelic beauty contrasted with the coldness with which she had participated in the crimes. The press dubbed them "Killer Barbie and Ken", a dark satire that highlighted the perverse nature hidden beneath a seemingly normal appearance.

22. The case of Lorena Bobbitt

The Lorena Bobbitt case became one of the most shocking media events of the 90s in the United States.

Lorena Bobbitt was born on October 31, 1970, in Ecuador and emigrated to the United States when she was a teenager. In June 1989, she met John Wayne Bobbitt, a former Marine and bartender, at a nightclub in Manassas, Virginia. Their relationship developed quickly and thcy married in June 1998.

The relationship between Lorena and John Bobbitt was tumultuous from the beginning. According to Lorena, John was violent and abusive, physically and emotionally. She claimed that he suffered repeated verbal and physical abuse during her marriage.

On June 23, 1993, the relationship reached a critical point. That night, after returning home from a night of work, Lorena alleged that John sexually violated her. After the alleged attack, Lorena went to the kitchen, where she grabbed an 8-inch kitchen knife.

In an act of desperation and anguish, Lorena cut off John Wayne Bobbitt's penis while he slept in his bed. She then left the house with the organ and drove for a few minutes before dumping it in a nearby field.

John Wayne Bobbitt woke up due to extreme pain and was rushed to the hospital. He underwent successful emergency surgery to reimplant his limb, and it became a notorious and sensational event throughout the country.

Lorena Bobbitt was arrested and charged with malicious castration. During her trial in 1994, her defense argued that she had acted under "transient insanity" due to the chronic abuse she had suffered at the hands of her husband. Witnesses testified about John's history of abuse towards Lorena and how this had affected her mental and emotional state.

The trial attracted widespread media attention and became a touchstone for debates about domestic violence and the justification of self-defense in cases of abuse. Ultimately, Lorena was acquitted of criminal charges due to temporary insanity.

Lorena Bobbitt's case highlighted the complexities of domestic violence cases and the difficult decision of abuse victims to protect themselves. It generated an intense public debate about gender violence and legal justice, as well as the ethics and sensationalism of the media in the coverage of sensitive cases.

After the trial, Lorena and John divorced in 1995. They both went their separate ways in life, and Lorena has stayed relatively out of the public eye since then.

23. The case of Dalia Dippolito

The Dalia Dippolito case is known to be an intriguing attempted murder plot that captured media attention in Florida, United States.

Dalia Dippolito was born on July 20, 1982, in New York. In 2009, she was married to Michael Dippolito, a businessman. Dalia had also previously been involved in minor legal problems, including fraud charges.

In May 2009, Dalia was arrested by Boynton Beach, Florida, police on charges of soliciting a hitman to murder her husband. The prosecution was based on video and audio evidence obtained during an undercover operation.

The case first came to light when Dalia's lover, Mohamed Shihadeh, informed police that Dalia was seeking to kill her husband. The police organized a sting operation, faking Michael's death to record Dalia's reaction. In the video, Dalia can be seen crying and reacting with false surprise to the news of her husband's death.

It was revealed that Dalia had contacted a supposed hitman, who was actually an undercover police agent. During their videotaped interactions, Dalia provided details about the location of the home, and Michael's schedule, and agreed to pay him $7,000 for the murder.

The motivations behind the assassination attempt were the subject of speculation. Some reports indicated that Dalia wanted the money from Michael's life insurance policy, while others suggested that she was looking for a way out of her marriage.

Dalia Dippolito's case became a highly publicized trial in 2011. During the trial, the defense argued that Dalia was being framed and that the undercover recordings were not sufficient evidence to prove her intention to commit the crime.

However, the prosecution presented compelling evidence, including video and audio recordings, that showed Dalia discussing the details of the murder with the undercover agent. The jury found Dalia Dippolito guilty of attempted murder in soliciting the death of her husband.

In 2011, she was sentenced to 20 years in prison. After a successful appeal in 2014, Ella Dippolito was subjected to a second trial in 2016, where she was again convicted of attempted murder. In July 2017, she received a 16-year prison sentence.

The case of Dalia Dippolito is a shocking example of the extremes to which betrayal and desperation can go in a marital relationship.

24. The case of Michele Williams

Michelle Williams was a 43-year-old woman from Keller, Texas, who was involved in a homicide case that shocked her community.

On the night of October 13, 2011, Michelle Williams called 911 reporting a burglary at her home. She claimed that an intruder had broken in, shot her husband, Greg Williams, and physically assaulted her. The crime scene showed Greg dead with a gunshot wound to the chest.

However, Michelle's story didn't add up. Investigations revealed inconsistencies in her story and forensic evidence suggested she had tampered with the crime scene. Additionally, the couple's friends and family described a troubled marriage, marked by arguments and domestic violence.

The investigation revealed that there were no intruders and Michele quickly changed her story, telling authorities that she made up the intruder story to try to cover up her husband's suicide and protect her daughter.

Michelle Williams was arrested and charged with murder. The trial became a media drama, with the defense pleading innocence and the prosecution presenting a strong case against them. The evidence included inconsistencies in Michelle's statements, the trail of blood that connected her to the crime scene, and the testimony of a neighbor who had heard her arguing with her husband shortly before her murder.

In 2014, after a two-week trial, Michelle Williams was found guilty of murder and tampering with evidence. The sentence was 30 years in prison, with the possibility of parole after 15 years.

The Michelle Williams case remains controversial. Some consider her a victim of domestic abuse who acted in self-defense, while others see her as a calculating murderer who manipulated justice.

25. The case of Jason Rohrer and Molly Martens

Jason Corbett was an Irish businessman, born in Limerick in 1976. He was a widower with two young children, Jack and Sarah. After the death of his first wife, Margaret "Mags" Fitzpatrick, in 2006, Jason was devastated. In 2008, he hired Molly Martens as a nanny for his children. Born in 1983, Molly was an American former model and tennis teacher from Knoxville, Tennessee. Over time, Jason and Molly's relationship evolved from a working relationship to a romantic one, and they married in 2011.

The relationship between Jason and Molly deteriorated over time. Testimony from friends and family suggested that there were significant tensions in the marriage. Jason, according to these testimonies, wanted to return to Ireland with his children, something that Molly was vehemently opposed to. Additionally, there were allegations that Molly was manipulative and that the relationship was characterized by conflict.

On August 2, 2015, police received a call from the Corbett-Martens residence in Davidson County, North Carolina. The call was placed by Tom Martens, Molly's father, a retired FBI agent. According to Tom, he had intervened in a fight between Jason and Molly and had hit Jason with a baseball bat in defense of himself and his daughter.

When police arrived at the scene, they found Jason Corbett dead in his bedroom. He had suffered multiple serious head injuries, inflicted by a baseball bat and a brick. Molly Martens and her father claimed that they had acted in her own defense, claiming that Jason had attacked Molly and that Tom intervened to protect her from her.

The investigation revealed inconsistencies in the statements of Molly and Tom Martens. Forensic experts found evidence suggesting Jason had been hit while he was in bed, contradicting claims of a fight in progress. Furthermore, no strong evidence was found that Jason had been aggressive or violent at the time of his death.

In 2017, Molly Martens and Tom Martens were put on trial for second-degree murder. During the trial, the prosecution argued that Jason's murder was premeditated and not an act of self-defense. Evidence was presented suggesting that Molly and Tom had planned the crime to prevent Jason from taking the children back to Ireland.

After a several-week trial, both were convicted of second-degree murder and sentenced to 20 to 25 years in prison.

In 2020, a North Carolina appeals court overturned the convictions of Molly and Tom Martens, arguing that errors had been made during the original trial that could have influenced the verdict. A new trial was ordered, bringing renewed attention to the case and controversy.

However, in June 2024, both were released on bail because they signed plea agreements.

Jason Corbett's family, particularly his children and his sister, have fought to preserve Jason's memory and ensure justice is served. The family has worked tirelessly to bring the children back to Ireland and provide them with a safe and loving environment, away from the trauma they experienced.

26. The case of Catherine Woods and Paul Cortez

Catherine Woods was a young and talented dancer born on June 8, 1983, in Columbus, Ohio. From an early age, she showed exceptional talent for dance and a strong desire to succeed in show business. Her parents supported her dream, and after graduating high school, Catherine moved to New York to pursue a career on Broadway.

Paul Cortez, born in 1979, also had big ambitions. He was an aspiring actor and musician who had studied at Harvard University. Cortez worked various jobs to support himself while he pursued his dream of acting and playing in rock bands in New York. It was in this vibrant and competitive city where Catherine and Paul crossed paths.

Catherine and Paul met in 2005 and began dating. However, their relationship was marked by ups and downs. Paul was jealous and possessive, and as Catherine's career began to take off, her insecurities grew. Catherine, for her part, was trying to balance her relationship with Paul and her increasing professional commitments.

On November 27, 2005, Catherine Woods was found dead in her apartment on 86th Street in Manhattan. She had been brutally murdered with multiple stab wounds to the neck. The crime scene was violent and suggested an impulsive, rage-filled attack.

The police were called by Catherine's roommate, who discovered her lying on the floor. News of her murder spread quickly, shocking the New York art community and her family in Ohio.

The police investigation initially focused on those closest to Catherine. Paul Cortez became a prime suspect due to his jealous behavior and his history of disturbing calls and emails directed at Catherine. Police also discovered that Paul had tried to contact her several times on the day of her death.

Forensic evidence played a crucial role in the case. Fingerprints and DNA found at the crime scene matched Paul Cortez. Furthermore, analysis of his mobile phone showed that he had been near Catherine's apartment at the time of the murder, despite his claims that he was elsewhere.

In November 2006, Paul Cortez was arrested and charged with the murder of Catherine Woods. The trial attracted a lot of media attention, with chilling details about the couple's relationship and the circumstances of the crime coming to light.

The prosecution argued that Paul Cortez, consumed by jealousy and anger, had killed Catherine in a violent attack after learning that she was seeing someone else. They presented DNA evidence, phone records, and testimony that painted Cortez as an obsessed and possessive man.

The defense attempted to argue that there was insufficient evidence to convict Cortez and suggested that someone else could have committed the crime. However, the weight of the forensic and circumstantial evidence was overwhelming.

In February 2007, Paul Cortez was convicted of second-degree murder and sentenced to 25 years to life in prison. The verdict brought some relief to Catherine's family, although the pain of losing her so tragically would never fully fade.

27. The case of Richard Crafts and Pamela Smart

Richard Crafts was an airline pilot and former member of the police, born in 1937 in New York. He married Helle Crafts (1947-1986), a Danish stewardess, in 1975. The couple lived in Newtown, Connecticut, and had three children. Although at first glance they seemed like a normal family, there were underlying problems in their marriage.

Over the years, the relationship between Richard and Helle became strained. Helle suspected that Richard was cheating on her and considered divorcing her. In 1986, Helle hired a private detective to investigate Richard's infidelities, and suspicions were confirmed.

On November 19, 1986, Helle Crafts disappeared. According to Richard, the last time he saw her was before a bad snowstorm. He said she had left the house to visit her sister in Denmark, but she never arrived.

Helle's friends and family worried about her when they didn't hear from her. The police began investigating and found several inconsistencies in Richard's story. Blood stains and other signs of violence were found in the Crafts' home.

The private detective Helle had hired provided crucial evidence, including photos of Richard with another woman and testimonies indicating his suspicious behavior.

The investigation revealed that Richard had used a wood chipper to dispose of Helle's body. The human remains found in the area where Richard had used the machine confirmed the worst fears.

In 1989, Richard Crafts was arrested and charged with murder. His trial, in 1990, was one of the first in the United States to convict someone without a complete body as evidence. He was found guilty and sentenced to 50 years in prison.

28. The Pamela Smart case

Pamela Ann Smart, born in 1967, was a media coordinator at a high school in New Hampshire. She married Gregg Smart in 1989. Pamela was known for being ambitious and charismatic, while Gregg was a quiet and hard-working man.

Pamela and Gregg's marriage began to deteriorate rapidly. Pamela, dissatisfied with her marital life, at 22 years old began a relationship with one of the students at the school where she worked, Billy Flynn, 15 years old.

On May 1, 1990, Gregg Smart was found dead in her home. He had been shot in the head. The crime scene initially suggested a botched robbery, but subsequent investigations revealed a much more sinister plot.

The police discovered that Pamela had convinced Billy Flynn and his friends to kill Gregg, promising that they would be together once Gregg was out of the way. The teenagers, influenced by Pamela, carried out the murder following her instructions.

Testimony from Billy's friends and recordings of incriminating conversations between Pamela and the teens provided irrefutable evidence.

In 1991, Pamela Smart was arrested and charged with conspiracy to commit murder. Her trial attracted widespread media attention and was broadcast live, becoming one of the first high-profile trials to be televised.

The case marked a milestone in the history of American criminal justice. It was the first trial to be broadcast live in its entirety. It was 1991. Every movement, every testimony, every detail was followed by millions of viewers.

Billy was released in 2015 after serving a 25-year sentence. Although Pamela Smart denied knowledge of the plot, she was convicted of being an accessory to first-degree murder and other crimes and sentenced to life in prison without parole.

29. The case of Kristen Clark and Robert Rovella

Kristen Clark was an attractive and ambitious young woman born in 1985. Known for her intelligence and determination, Kristen moved to Phoenix, Arizona, after college in hopes of starting a career in marketing. She was a people person and quickly formed a circle of friends in her new surroundings.

Robert Rovella, born in 1979, was a charismatic and charming man who worked in sales. Robert had a magnetic personality that attracted those around him and was known for his ability to persuade and his lavish lifestyle.

Kristen and Robert met at a party in mid-2011. The connection was instant, and they soon began a passionate relationship. Despite differences in age and lifestyle, their romance blossomed quickly.

As the relationship progressed, Kristen and Robert faced several problems. Kristen discovered that Robert had a history of manipulative and dishonest financial behavior. Robert, for his part, was jealous and controlling, which caused tensions in their relationship.

Kristen began to suspect that Robert was hiding something more sinister. Her erratic behavior and constant lies about her job and her finances made her feel increasingly insecure.

On February 10, 2012, Kristen Clark disappeared without a trace. Her family and friends worried about her not hearing from her, as it was unusual for her not to communicate.

Police launched an investigation and found Kristen's car abandoned in a parking lot near her apartment. There were no signs of a struggle, but the discovery of her car was disturbing.

On February 15, 2012, Kristen's body was found in a desert area outside of Phoenix. She had been brutally beaten and strangled. The crime scene indicated that it had been a violent and premeditated murder.

The investigation quickly focused on Robert Rovella. Police discovered that there were several inconsistencies in his alibi for the night of Kristen's disappearance. Additionally, they found threatening text messages that Robert had sent her shortly before her disappearance.

Detectives also discovered that Robert had a history of violent behavior and financial scams. There were several allegations from former partners and business associates that described a pattern of manipulation, deceit, and violence.

In May 2012, Robert Rovella was arrested and charged with the murder of Kristen Clark. During the trial, the prosecution presented compelling evidence including threatening text messages, testimony from witnesses who saw Robert near where Kristen's body was found, and forensic analysis linking Robert to the crime scene.

The defense attempted to argue that there was no direct evidence linking Robert to the murder and suggested that he may have been the victim of a violent robbery by unknown persons. However, the weight of evidence and witness testimony disproved this theory.

In December 2012, Robert Rovella was convicted of first-degree murder and sentenced to life in prison without the possibility of parole.

30. The case of Susan Hamilton

Susan Hamilton was a well-known dermatologist in Oklahoma City, described by her colleagues and patients as a woman dedicated and passionate about her work. Susan was married to John Hamilton, a respected obstetrician and gynecologist. They had met in 1985 when he was 37 and she was 39 years old. The couple was known in their community for being successful and apparently happy.

At first glance, John and Susan Hamilton seemed to have an ideal marriage. However, like many couples, they faced underlying issues that were not evident to others. John was known for being a loving and attentive man, while Susan was described as a loving wife. However, tensions arose in their relationship, especially around John's infidelities and controlling behavior.

On February 14, 2001, on Valentine's Day, John Hamilton found his wife dead in his home. According to his story, John had left Susan at home that morning to attend surgery at the hospital. Upon returning, he found Susan brutally beaten and strangled in the master bathroom of her home. John immediately called 911 but attempts to revive Susan were in vain.

The police launched a thorough investigation. Although it initially appeared that John was devastated by the death of his wife, suspicions began to arise about his possible involvement in the crime. Investigators found several inconsistencies in his account and discovered evidence suggesting that John had been unfaithful to Susan, which could have caused conflict in their marriage.

Forensic evidence was crucial in this case. Blood stains found on John's clothing and body, as well as the lack of signs of forced entry into the house, heightened suspicions. Additionally, the crime scene showed signs of a violent struggle, indicating that Susan had tried to defend herself.

John Hamilton was arrested and charged with the murder of his wife. The trial attracted widespread media attention due to the brutality of the crime and the public nature of the couple. The prosecution argued that John, in a fit of rage and jealousy, had killed Susan after an argument over her infidelities.

The defense tried to argue that John had no motive to kill his wife. However, the forensic evidence and testimony presented by the prosecution were compelling. In 2002, John Hamilton was convicted of first-degree murder and sentenced to life in prison without the possibility of parole.

The murder of Susan Hamilton on Valentine's Day is a heartbreaking case of a crime of passion that exposes the depths of betrayal and domestic violence. The life of a talented and successful woman was tragically cut short by the anger of her husband, leaving a trail of pain and devastation in her community.

-----0-----

If you want to continue reading about more amazing facts and data that the author has collected; We invite you to immerse yourself in reading the following titles found on this platform:

- The biggest conspiracy theories

- Great heists in history

- Famous murderers - the perverse side of the mind -

- Lives in captivity –Stories of real kidnappings-

- Agents, informants and traitors - the world of espionage -

- Pirates of the 21st century

- Tragic loves